RESERVED WORDS AND COMMENTS

A COMMUNICATIONS ART HANDBOOK

JANE SUMMERS

AuthorHouse™
1663 Liberty Drive
Bloomington, IN 47403
www.authorhouse.com
Phone: 833-262-8899

Because of the dynamic nature of the Internet, any web addresses or links contained in this book may have changed since publication and may no longer be valid. The views expressed in this work are solely those of the author and do not necessarily reflect the views of the publisher, and the publisher hereby disclaims any responsibility for them.

Any people depicted in stock imagery provided by Getty Images are models, and such images are being used for illustrative purposes only.
Certain stock imagery © Getty Images.

This book is printed on acid-free paper.

Library of Congress Control Number: 2022911510
ISBN: 978-1-6655-6308-6 (sc)
ISBN: 978-1-6655-6309-3 (e)

Print information available on the last page.

Published by AuthorHouse 07/20/2022

authorHOUSE®

CONTENTS

ACKNOWLEDGEMENTS

This book is dedicated to my father Dr. Chinta Chidananda Rao (Chief Medical Officer, South Central Railway), my mother Chinta Visalakshi, my husband Srinivas Madiraju, my daughter Anika Madiraju, my family and friends.

My sincere appreciation to all my friends, and well-wishers who have helped me at all times.

Reserved Words and Comments, is a 25-chapter book of communication skill essays, and shows the different ways a word or a comment must be reserved for communication in any setting. This book is targeted to readers for a value of communication skill acquired as an art for a purpose.

Reserved Words and Comments can be used by one to track words and comments in any setting for success and growth. The reader must have a dictionary of words and comments for use in corporate and other settings. The book underlies the theory of reservation of words and comments that words and comments must be constrained and limited by one, if it results in negative outcomes.

Part 1 - Reserved Words and Comments

1
CHAPTER

RESERVED WORDS AND COMMENTS

RESERVED WORDS AND COMMENTS, A DEFINITION

Reservation is a concept associated with several words that we use as action verbs to restrict or prohibit an action or activity for a purpose. The purpose can range from restriction of an activity for a social, personal or others, or restriction of law for a rule to prohibit one from committing an activity not correct according to rules and regulation enacted by law, to contain the boundary of an activity for restriction.

A reserved an activity for a business purpose must include words or comments for communication that are used as goals or strategies for fulfillment of an objective for a purpose of a business. Goals in a personal life can be extended to a social or organizational environment to include a restriction of a boundary for an activity not to violate a personal or family fulfillment.

Comments is a word that can be associated with several action adjectives or adverbs. Reserved words and comments is an art or a style that must be chosen by a person or an organization for fulfillment of a concrete positive goal for a purpose positive and for an outcome positive.

Reserved words is a restriction of words that must not be spoken and not used if it hinders the progress to a path of education, work, business or for a personal or family purpose. A reserved a word or a comment can be defined as words or sentences that contain words that must not be communicated for either a business, personal or family purpose that disrupts the path to progress and causes a failure in a result such as education, marriage, work, organization and in other areas of life.

A second side of the coin of reservation is a reserved words positive that must be used as powerful action verbs or adverbs for a goal fulfillment of a mission statement or a strategy implementation in a business for success through progress and growth.

Every communication, a reserved word or comment, written or verbal, is an interaction between parties for an outcome. We need to define these words of communication as an agreement between parties for an interaction of a meeting, and comments from these communications as restrictions within the boundaries of communication, to be viewed as continuity for use of words as a medium of communication for an outcome of an interaction or an agreement positive and not otherwise.

2

CHAPTER

RESERVED WORDS AND COMMENTS

WORDS AND SENTENCES - A VALUE OF FULFILLMENT FOR A PURPOSE

Words that are reserved and cannot be used for a negativity of goal fulfillment include verbs and adverbs such as not, cannot, is not, aren't, will not and others. Expressions of negativity must be excluded for a path of progress in personal, family, work and others. Words and expressions of negativity will hinder the path of progress by aggregating thoughts that are not positive and accumulating reasons for negativity of an interaction increasing a bias on one side, for each reservation word or comment used for fulfillment of an interaction for fulfillment of an agreement, positive.

A communication skill is an art and a style for any a reserved a word for communication that will translate a word or a sentence to a meaningful action for a fulfillment of a purpose, and the purpose must only include words or comments that are positive for a positive outcome of a person, group, organization and others.

A reserved a word or a comment must not include words or comments that are coarse, rude, vulgar, cruel, brutal that are negative words for a communication and an interaction of people in a family, school, company, organizational setting, and others.

A reserved a word or a comment communicated poorly can cause a negative impact and a ripple effect on the minds of all or any for a lifetime. Such words and comments for reservation must be contained at every level and reservation restriction applied through mentoring, coaching at a lower level and, through enforcement of laws that are rigid for activities such as destruction contained through a boundary of law, for offenses and crimes at the personal, family, organizational and other levels at a higher level.

Reserved words or sentences adopted from books that are not recommended for the young and old and for ages at all levels must be restricted and prohibited enacted as laws by any an organization for a purpose, as it will cause a negative impact on the age groups of all. Such reserved words and comments must be simulated using positive outcomes for a result positive through examples of positive exercises of all ages.

Reserved words and sentences as a communication viewed on the screen, tv or theaters that are cruel and brutal must be strictly prohibited at all levels as it may cause an impact in the personal, family, work, and organization levels. Such values are instilled in the mind of one through views of others and implemented causing a severe destruction in areas such as education, family and work life. Children and adults follow the same pattern of communication with no respect between individuals such as respect of a child for a parent restricting the growth patterns or progress of a child in a family life, break up of family relationships with no boundary restriction on words and comments. Kids are orphaned with no one to care for them resulting in criminal sentences of kids for reform, and impacting the minds of the young at an early age hindering the continuity for success in all areas of life.

The manifestations of words or expressions from any a source is viewed and enacted in schools, college, work or other areas. Such profiles are portrayed and shown as characters of hero in a setting and the profile adopted by others. There are other types of words used through approaches and gestures that do not bring respect for virtues of values or for a code of conduct and discipline met. Such words can cause aggressive behavior through use of loud voices resulting in violence. Reserved words and comments must be manifested through use of a ready book or use of a class of ready words and behavior for reserved words and comments to contain words and comments through boundaries of reservation.

Words and comments violating use of restriction of words and comments are sentences used by any and become the habit of one to continuously adopt this approach for a resolution of an outcome(s) a lifetime. The resolution of words and comments for containment is to create a process for elimination of wastage of words and comments for an outcome through an improvement process for use of words and comments for a purpose through a lean mixed methodology pattern of words and comments used and received well for every scenario. Some examples are, a peace and harmony not implemented at the family level is reflected through an aggressive approach for use of words and comments used in the work environment causing a negative impact on a person, a group, an organization or others.

3
CHAPTER

RESTRICTION OF WORDS AND COMMENTS AT FAMILY LEVEL

RESERVATION A CAUSE AND VALUE FOR A REASON AND VALUE ONLY POSITIVE

Reserved words and comments in a family setting is a value that brings the profile of a family member to public visibility such as for family interactions, work, school and other settings. A value of a word is a symbol of a character profile and stands for a value of respect, appreciation, grace and other virtues and these values are weighed for values of harmony and peace in addition to other virtues of values.

Reserved words and comments must be defined for a family through a dictionary of use by a family at all times, and must continue to be a family dictionary and a dictionary for all for emulation. Such a dictionary must include creation of new words in places such as in school, college, university, work and also at the organizational level for positive outcomes of growth in all areas of life of every.

An organization at a higher level must administer rules to reserve words and comments for use within and outside a setting. Words not restricted must include adjectives for praise, hard work, sincerity, devotion, grace, loyalty, peace and harmony. All these virtues of values must be embodied as virtues of a person when a profile is created and assembled. These value virtues must be met through goals defined using strategies identified at different levels of progression for growth at every setting and every level.

Reserved words and comments must include a word for not to speak or an expression not to use to devalue any in any a setting. These words and expressions will not open avenues in life for progression to newer relationships or to grow existing relations to help increase positive values of life for an attitude of helpfulness, compassion, consideration, and support for an enthusiasm and eagerness to support any a positive outcome in life.

A communication skill for words and comments must include a list of words, sentences and expressions, for use at every level for a progression of virtue of values of growth in all areas of life.

4

CHAPTER

RESERVED WORDS AND COMMENTS

ISOLATION FOR CONTAINMENT OF WORDS AND SENTENCES - A VALUE OF PROGRESS FOR VIRTUES

Reserved words and comments for a purpose and a setting level must be identified through isolation of a list of words translated to sentences for a purpose that cannot be used for any others unless for a purpose such as for a specific scenario. A quarrel to be set aside for a transition to a state of peace and harmony, a negative relationship for a positive relation such as at work, a social setting, a marriage or others where people do not use words or comments for a value of mutual benefit for peace and harmony.

Reserved words and comments must rest on the premise of peaceful coexistence for interactions and communication at every level and setting such as in a personal, family, work, social, group or organizational setting level.

Reserved words and comments must not only include the above scenarios but also words and sentences that will not only improve relationships at the family level for a continuity of support, loyalty, peace, harmony, friendship and trust but also increase the value virtues at other levels with time. Such words for reserved words and comments to be avoided at every level include, dislike, not, never, no, cannot, do not, will never, against, will not, don't know, not favorable and others. These words will build an opinion of a value for devalue such as to ignore, defeat, rebel, fight, and other actions of negative impact in the minds of the receiver, and may result in the loss of a family relationship, a loss of job, a loss of marriage and others.

A reserved word and comment for a value of progress must be the only reason for a source and a want for a word use, and the only use for a means to an end positive. These words must include a value of progress for laughter for a continuity of any a positive outcome, renewal of friendships to fulfill goals such as in education, work and others for a value of progress. Other examples of reserved words and comments include a social interaction for a growth that resulted in acquiring high intellectual profile for new value growth opportunities at school, work, and other areas.

Reserved words and comments in other areas for value acquisition include new words and sentences that will generate value for new subjects to promote scientific and engineering intelligence for invention and innovation, promote growth for new entrants pursuing new avenues of education and work for growth, a value progress using value virtue methodology.

Reserved comments and words negative must include silence, a value for not to receive and send a communication to another for fear of not moving towards progress or growth, a goal for fulfillment. Actions to delivery for a positive outcome for comments is also a preferred virtue value in some cases to generate appreciation or progress measured by the receiving party through performance evaluated for accomplishment met and exceeded for goals fulfilled at different levels of setting of any.

5
CHAPTER

RESERVED WORDS AND COMMENTS

RESERVATION, A VALUE OF FUTURE AGGREGATIONS

A reservation we aggregate over a period of time, is a virtue value we assign using a score to generate a future value stream for a value stream of communications that are communications through interactions weighed and measured for a value positive or negative over a period of time benchmarked using comparison metrics to generate value.

A value for a value stream communication is a value generated based on a goal fulfillment for a value met at any setting such as at family, education, work, social organizational and other levels.

The words used and contained through reserved words and comments for use is based on per util for an interaction of a communication sent and received. A value stream communication is positive and is an aggregation if the communication stream through the interaction received is a positive util for a series of positive utils over a period of time to measure a path of progress for growth, for a value computed for renewal of a future value benefit.

Reserved words and comments is an indicator of growth metrics, (KPI metrics) used as a measure for a value of a reserved a word and comment constrained not for a utilization or a use and computed as a metric based on optimization metric technique. Some examples of reserved words and comments for use include a job continuity with no job loss, a job promotion for an increase in salary and responsibility, an increase in credibility of trust and loyalty of an employee, increased skill and growth using innovation and invention through training and skill acquisition of a job by an employee for continued growth and others.

6

CHAPTER

RESERVED WORDS
AND COMMENTS

A CONTAINMENT, A RESTRICTION ONLY FOR AN OPTIMIZATION

A reserved words and comments for a containment for optimization of virtue value must include words that serve as pre-cautioned words such as, before I say, implications of a word (a thread of conversation), results of a discussion (a negative evaluation), consequences of an action (not use of tease words for an interaction) and others that will help serve as measures of optimization techniques for a containment of words and comments for reserved words and comments not for use.

A reserved a word and comment optimization technique includes: a difference of a value positive earned for a period of time measured using a containment or a constraint methodology technique, a communication exchange of a value received for a value met of an interaction (verified for value), a reserved a word and comment isolated and not for a use or misuse for any a purpose, a reserved a word and comment overridden with new value words that are virtue value and others.

Reserved words and comments for contempt, or tease (words such as mimicking a character, not a grace, words such as fool, idiot, shame) should not be part of vocabulary at home, school, education, university or at work level for progress or growth to a higher level of intellect at every level of interaction for a promotion to a different level of value earned.

Other reservation words and comments that must be set aside for new virtue values include identification of new words for new respect, appreciation for a new way of communication, and actions met with words together for a synonym and an attribute value met for a rule met.

Reservations of words and comments is a communication skill that must be mastered at every level and reviewed through virtue value metrics for use of words at family, education, work and other levels of setting.

Reserved words and comments at the organizational level includes containment of words at the cultural level for differences of words in communication for use and meaning not to cause a negative outcomes. The value difference of use of words and comments for an interaction of communication must be to use words that renew a communication for new interactions in every setting. A value difference of words or comments for a containment value must be defined based on reserved words and comments rule criteria for a virtue value of a word or comment value earned.

7

CHAPTER

RESERVED WORDS
AND COMMENTS

RESERVATION A CAUSE AND EFFECT, A VIRTUE VALUE METHODOLOGY

Reserved words and comments used after an interaction must be reviewed and new solutions and new words identified for negative outcomes through assembling of new words and comments using word streams and word presses. These néw set of word streams and word presses must be categorized under new headers called word stream rule based words and comments for use and improvements for a word or use must include replacement of existing words and comments with new words based on failure scenarios.

Reserved words and comments must use a theory based analysis for a cause and effect identification using review of word streams process after an interaction of communication. The reserved words and comments based analysis uses constructs theory identification for realignment of a word mismatch to a new word alignment for positive outcome. An example is a 'Need a new rule' theory based on negative outcome of a word or comment and to discontinue, for a new word for use and renewal of an existing word for an outcome positive.

A new cause and effect reserved word and comment theory includes use of new constructs using titles for an abstract, and theory for an analysis of reconstruction of a new reserved word and comment interaction using new word streams or word presses of an interaction for a purpose. Such analysis is based on a statement or a word driven rule based criteria, using communication interaction scenarios for a use and a purpose, and an implementation for a positive result. These values are aggregated through word stream and word press measures and evaluated for progress based on the interactions aggregated for new scores from revisions, for reuse until scores result in an optimal value.

A reserved words and comments methodology must include a reserved word construct and a stream of key words for an interaction for a list of objectives to be met for an interaction(s) for a purpose. Such a methodology must be reviewed and tested through a pilot study for a progress of virtue values from an interaction or a series of interactions and the scores measured using a metric measure of reserved words and comments methodology optimization metrics.

8

RESERVED WORDS AND COMMENTS

WORD PRESS A VALUE OF WORD STREAM FOR AN INTERACTION OF A COMMUNICATION EFFECTIVE

A reserved a word and comment for a score calculation must include key words and comments used as word streams for a communication from an interaction, for a purpose fulfilled or renewed for a positive score and a purpose failed and not renewed for a negative score.

Reserved words and comments must include a stream of words using word press identification method as a strategy for an interaction of a communication. The words need to be cumulated and aggregated for an outcome positive or negative and a virtue value benefit generated from the outcome of such an interaction. Such word streams of communication can be gathered using a word press collection mechanism and put together as a word press collection of words identified for a need and purpose of an interaction.

Reserved words and comments for communication are abstracted and indexed using a reserved word dictionary index based approach for a word search for a word or a sentence for a purpose and delivery of a communication. Such dictionaries are similar to other dictionaries except that they can be used for communication through interactions for effective use and reuse of words for a purpose and goal fulfillment from a communication(s). The indexed words must be categorized using a moon chart, circular, for a purpose, a mission and a strategy for a communication style using effective word stream communication mechanism, a skill for an art and style of communication.

A communication stream is a stream of reserved words used for a purpose of an interaction, measured and cut based on the length of an interaction, time span of an interaction, and the number of words needed for a word stream communication, for an interaction. These words streams can also be extended using additional words or word streams using a question and answer approach for a realization of a virtue value from an interaction.

Reserved words and comments of a word press can be accommodated using a criteria based rule generator for a personal, business, and others. Such word presses can resemble a shape such as a pattern for a grouping, a symmetry for an attribute(s), an asymmetry for opposites that need to identified for a new grouping or extension, and others.

Reserved words and comments of words streams and word presses can also be created using visual identification approaches to create new patterns of rules based on naturalistic patterns derived from nature or from a book, reviewed and assembled to create new word streams of communication. Such word streams can be assembled using a disquisition (comprehensive) based approach for an effective communication style, an art met for a virtue value of communication.

9

CHAPTER

RESERVED WORDS AND COMMENTS

GOAL ACHIEVERS IN A COLLABORATIVE ROLE OF INCREASED RESPONSIBILITY

Reserved words and comments measured and evaluated for a goal(s) met consecutively by any are goal achievers and leaders of new knowledge and serve as mentors and coaches for a collaborative role translated to a role of leadership based on the communication interactions received of word streams. The use of reserved words and comments acquired from such collaborators serve as additional knowledge avenues, to build new knowledge streams for effective communication style for an interaction(s).

Reserved words and comments is a source of knowledge I need to extract for a knowledge acquisition or a knowledge translation using a reserved word and comment optimization tool for an effective word stream communication, to exceed a goal for fulfillment of an effective communication style. A mastery of such a reserved word and comments tool will help one to move to a new role of promotion in the work area, or to a higher intellectual level in the education area and other categories.

A communication word stream flow I create and implement and a feedback I receive is a progress I measure for a difference of a virtue value positive from an interaction, and an appreciation and respect I gather for a communication style at any a level, evaluated not only for the communication style, but also for the new knowledge acquisition of a topic of disquisition(s).

Reserved words and comments is measured for every interaction either in a home, educational, corporate or other settings. A new way to search new word streams for effective communication styles include review of emails, news, subjects, and others for a purpose of either a reply, a new word sentence creation for a new subject topic or others. Such type of word streams as a communication style serve as tools that set the path for a tone and a note of innovation and invention for new word streams of communication using an effective communication style. Such word streams also help generate values of word streams to identify and assemble new topics in different subject areas for a purpose(s).

The path to a successful interaction of a communication can also take the form of a team consensus received from a social interaction or other categories for a period of time, not challenged or failed for a goal of a purpose met. Reserved words and comments serve as a path to a success for role fulfillment in all areas of life using an effective word stream communication style as an art for a communication approach for an outcome positive.

10

CHAPTER

RESERVED WORDS AND COMMENTS - A DAY OF WORK!

SEVERAL RESERVED WORDS AND COMMENTS I COLLECTED AND USED FOR A WORD STREAM - AN IMPACT ANALYSIS

An Impact of reserved words and comments is a measure I collected and used for word streams of several interactions over several periods. Each interaction is a result of a word stream I used and the feedback I collected over a period. A measure complete of an interaction through a communication style of reserved words and comments met is a goal met, a score of 95-100 out of 100 for every interaction using the reserved words and comments communication approach for an outcome positive of a goal met and exceeded.

An impact of an interaction using reserved words and comments communication for a discussion is a gain if the outcome of such an interaction results in a positive benefit such as a gain, and not for a re-initiation of a discussion or a deadlock for not to move forward.

An impact analysis of reserved words and comments includes several informational exercises generated from an interaction for a purpose such as for a calculated score of a communication style, a re-definition of a word stream of a communication style, a revision of a summary using the reserved word stream communication style and others. A new definition of an interaction using reserved words and comments approach is a value generated for use of a strength of a word stream for a focus, delivery and an outcome and impact positive.

An impact negative of a word or a word stream must be deleted or put in a category not for use, and archived as wasted. A negative metric will be used to weigh the value for a use vs not for use for a virtue value of a reserved word and comment category. Such word streams of reserved words and comments must be identified for removal from the dictionary of reserved words using the reserved words and comments rule based methodology.

Please refer to reserved words and comments methodology in the next chapter.

11
CHAPTER

RESERVED WORDS AND COMMENTS

COMMENTS AS FEEDBACK FOR ANALYSIS

Comments is a word, a one line statement, a paragraph, a note or a disquisition(s). The source of such comments can come from either emails, a grade response from a school or university, a work performance result, a workplace comment from discussions during meetings, team and scrum discussion interactions, and others.

Comments can originate from a supervisor such as a Professor, a Boss and others. Comments can also originate from an employee, a student or others in a lower rank. Comments in all situations must be reserved within a boundary for positive and negative responses to include every communication for an interaction.

Comments must be assembled using a case communication methodology rule framework with a title, date, comment, a discussion paragraph, listed, analyzed, reviewed using examples from books of successful responses, or other sources and replaced with positive responses for comments met for an interaction of communication.

Comments must be evaluated for a positive or a negative response through a comment rule based methodology for a thread of conversation received for a topic and arranged under conversation headers for every conversation received to prevent duplication of conversation topics. A request and response for a communication must be saved together as a thread using the case communication methodology framework, and each recurrence for a conversation of the same topic must be saved with subtitles under the main thread of communication topic.

Comments include reserved words for interactions of communications. Such comments include reserved words for a verbal use, a speech, or a written response received or requested as a comment for an interaction of communication. Comments for a positive or a negative response must be identified, critiqued and evaluated through literature review, and listed with synonyms for a best use of an interaction for communication using the points to synonym technique for optimal use.

Comments for optimal use in every case scenario must be evaluated and pilot tested through a case based scenario approach for a communication thread for a request and response, and new revisions made using new values of virtues of word streams communication patterns using communication based pattern approach.

Optimal use scenarios for a reserved word and comment communication methodology include pattern based communication approaches such as a circular based communication approach, a linear based communication approach, an angular based communication approach, a mind-mapping based communication approach and others.

12
CHAPTER

RESERVED WORDS AND COMMENTS

The reserved words and comments methodology is explained through a few examples of the methodology for a criteria met of a process for an interaction of communication of any for a goal fulfillment.

Score is computed from an interaction of communication through criteria and literature review for goal fulfillment. The literature review of the company or organization is for an additional support of the goal fulfillment met for an acceptance criteria. The following examples explain the reserved word and comment communication methodology through case scenarios for goal fulfillment.

1. **Compare Critique Methodology:** The Compare Critique reserved word communication and comment methodology lists scenarios not Met for a criteria determined for goal fulfillment and not supported through literature review for goal fulfillment. The methodology is used to create a reserved word and comment communication case rule based on acceptance criteria and literature support for goal fulfillment accepted by the customer. Please see below for an example of the compare critique methodology of reserved words and comments.

2. **Points to Synonym Method**

3. **Identification of Reserved words**

List the words for a value virtue of a process for an interaction of a communication based on Reserved Word and Comments methodology

Part 2 - Jane Summers Poetry Classics

A friend,
My family!

An autumn,
My oak tree,
The first days,
Unable to
Weather the breeze,
A mid-autumn,
Empty,
Only standing alone,
A dew,
Unable to see,
My oak tree
I cannot see,
An occasional peek,
Until A breeze,
An end,
Only a summer!
My Oak tree,
A grace,
All seasons,
I respect and trust,
My true friend!

MY AUTUMN EGGPLANT COLORS!

Water drops,
A few,
An eggplant,
A purple deep,
Afresh, a farm,
Smiling,
A corner,
My basket,
A yellow,
And a deep purple, eggplants,
Several,
Only for sunrise colors,
A painting in my kitchen,
A match,
A sunset, colors and shape,
My purple,
And yellow,
Autumn eggplants,
I feel safe,
Visible,
Only my home!

THE SUMMER GARDEN!

A summer garden,
Flowers, light,
Leaves, clear, a color,
A wave of hands,
Flowers and leaves
Smiles, of a summer garden!
Every, a, flower, a profile,
Clear, a grace,
A beauty,
Of a face,
A wisdom,
Of An appearance,
Only for an appreciation, any,
Every a season!

Leaves, a branch, a
Profile,
A grace, I carry,
A profile of an ancestry!

A FIRST MUM, AN AUTUMN DAY!

My mums,
Several colors, An autumn,
A color deep,
A difference a summer?
Colors, a few more,
An autumn!
My autumn colors of my mums,
A match an autumn color only,
Of an autumn!
A blend, a purple and orange,
An autumn sunrise,
A color, a visitor for a short time,
My mums, colors deep,
Only a visitor, until a winter!

A first of an autumn day,
Farms, afar,
Lines, several colors,
My mums,
Arranged in baskets,
And carts,
Pumpkins, orange,
In my autumn farms,
Heralding the arrival,
Of an autumn!
A symbol!
Patches of
Pumpkins, an orange
And
Mums,
Green, yellow, brown, orange,
Colors of my autumn leaves,
A carpet on the ground,
A match of
My autumn mum colors!

Part 3 - Jane Summers
Piano Classics

DURVUE SONGS

An Autumn Sacred

Auve Aumovue sacovue!
B5 middle black key left a5g5f5e5

Mivue Daouven Ovue Aumovue!
B5 middle black key left a5g5f5e5d5c5

Novue Anovue!
B5 black key left a5g5

Aue Tiouve!
B5 black key left a5g5

Tovue Misouve!
B5 black key left a5g5

Auve Arouve!
B5 black key left a5g5

Lesouve, auve davovue!
a5g5f5e5d5

Aue Daovuen Forovue!
B5 black key left a5g5f5e5d5

Auve Amouve Sacavoue
B5 a5g5f5e5d5c5

Aue Amouve pravavuen sacauve!

Amouve Amouve Sacavoue
a5g5f5e5d5
U
Sacavoue auve prauvuen anouv amouve

Prayers of Peace
Middle keys

Prayers of peace
pravavuen ovue peaucue!
C5-A5
Peace, my prayers of sunrise,

Peauce mivue Pravavuen
ovue, suverwei!
A5-c5; c5; ded:
A sunrise, a blessing!
Aue suwervei, besauvue!
Cded: Ed!

Prayers, Every!
Prauvuen overvuew!
Cde,edd;
Peace, A harmony!
Peauce, avue, harmoivuew!
Ed;c;edcd

Peace, my living!
Peauce, mivue, levauvew!
A5-C5

GERMAN SONG

B#A5G5
Freunde für Tage
B#A5G5
Freunde ein paar
eine Familie fürs Leben
A5-E5
A family I need, a peace a life
Left E4-D4 ; D4
Eine Familie, die ich ein Leben lang zum ein Frieden brauche
Left E4-B5
Eine Familie, die ich ein Leben lang für eine Harmonie brauche
C5-E5 2 times E5D5C5

Freunde, wir sind
Family we are!
Familie wir sind
Eine familie fürs Leben

B#A5G5
Freunde für Tage
B#A5G5
Freunde ein paar
eine Familie fürs Leben
A5-E5

Eine Familie, die ich zum trost brauche
Eine Familie, die ich eine zuhause brauche
A family, a friend precious, a lifetime!
Ein Freund, mein familie!
Ein freund, mein zuhause
Eine freund fürs Leben

Freunde, wir sind
Family we are!
Familie wir sind
Eine Familie fürs Leben

Wunderbar mein freunde
Sehr schon ein trost!
Sehr wunderbar ein trost!

Sehr gluckliche ein trost

Freunde, wir sind
Familie wir sind
eine Familie fürs Leben

B#A5G5
Freunde für Tage
B#A5G5
Freunde ein paar
eine Familie fürs Leben
A5-E5

AUTUMN SACRED - MUSICAL ALBUM 2

1.   Autumn Promises

Autumn, Autumn,
Ed, Ed
A Prayer, an autumn!
Edc, edc
A promise, an autumn,
Dcbag
Sacred an autumn!
C#d#f#g#A#g#
A prayer, a promise, an autumn, I fulfill!
Dcbagfed

Autumn, my promises, a few
C#d#; f#g#a#
Autumn, a new Season, a new day
C#d#, f#g#a#
Autumn a new line, a new prayer
C#d#, f#g#a#

An autumn, a season, a prayer, I fulfill!
A#g#f#; a#g#f#; a#g#f#;d#c#d#

Autumn, Autumn,
D# c# d# c#
how far, a season?
A#g#f#d#c#
Autumn Autumn
How deep, how true, how new a color?

Autumn autumn,
A prayer, a season, a name new,
Autumn autumn how many?
A new name, a line new, a prayer
A new art, a new autumn, I bestow
A season, an Autumn , a prayer I fulfill!

My violets, my Roses, my daisies
I bestow!
My panchamrutam, a festival
An aautumn, I bestow!

My beads, a tradition,
An autumn a season a prayer I fulfill!

Autumn promises part2

Autumn , a dream true,
An autumn,
Gold a flower, I shower,
Silver I bestow,
My prayers, A sunrise,
C#d#d#; f#g#a#
My beads, my art, my thoughts, my tradition,an autumn!

C#d#; f#g#a#
my gems, my art!
C#d#; f#g#a#

An autumn,
A prayer, a season,
I fulfill!
A#g#f#; a#g#f#; a#g#f#; c#d#c#

An autumn my Sacred
C#d#; f#g#a#
An autumn My melody
C#d#; f#g#a#
An autumn my grace!
C#d#; f#g#a#
Autumn autumn how true a season!

An autumn,autumn,
A prayer,
A season,
An autumn, I fulfill
A#g#f#; a#g#f#; a#g#f#; c#d#c#
Autumn my violets,
Autumn, my mums
Autumn, my Roses,

Autumn, my mums, a violet!
Autumn my mums a rose!
Autumn my mums, a daisy!
An autumn, a prayer
—A flower, a season, I celebrate!
A season I celebrate!
Autumn! Autumn Autumn

Autumn! Autumn
Autumn!
A prayer, an autumn!

2. An Autumn quest

A smile I cherish a life time,
An art I remember, seasons!

Grace, seasons,
Days of smiles,
Days of art,
Days of autumn,
Seasons, An autumn, true!

Days of autumn,
Wither a leaf, I see!
Days of autumn
dew, my door, a view!
Days of autumn,
Warmth, a color, a season!
Comfort, a season, an autumn!

A prayer, I remember a lifetime,
A grace, a season, an autumn, true!

home, a warmth, my tradition!
Togetherness, a harmony, a day,
Days of clouds, an art
Days of autumn, a color!
peace my living, A truth!

Seasons, I remember your smile,every!
A face, a portrait, I cherish, a lifetime!
True seasons,
words, my songs
Songs a carve,
Art, my devotion, an autumn!

Bespoke autumn!
Truth an autumn!
Seasons an autumn!
An autumn, peace, my living, true!

3. Autumn A walk of a season!

Purple, blue, a color, my autumn!
Green brown, a color, my autumn leaf!
My autumn days,
A# G# AG
My autumn walk,
A# G# AG
 a day
a difference, true!
AGFE

Sunrise true!
D# c b
Sunset true!
D# c b
Age, a leaf, an autumn!
Dcbagfedc

An autumn walk, an autumn day,
a grace, a color true!
Sunrise true
Sunset true,
A day of harmony true!

Orange brown, a color my autumn sunrise!
Grey pink, a color, my autumn sunset!

Summers true!
Autumn true!
Awake, a spring, a new Flower!

My autumn breeze,
My autumn walk,
A sunrise, a difference, true!

Sunrise bells
Sunset bells
A day of an autumn blessing!

Orange, red
Purple, red
Orange pink
Orange green
A grace of an autumn season!

4.   An ode to autumn

Hills of autumn
D#d#; fe
A praise of autumn
D#d#d# fe
An ode to an autumn !
D# d# d# fe

Grace a praise of trust and truth!
Bagfg
Days, a season sacred and true!
Bagfg!
Days, an autumn red and yellow!
Bagfeg!

Prayers, an ode to autumn hills!
E;eeeeef!
Tradition, an ode of an autumn temple!
E: eeeeeef!

Autumn, a rock I worship thee!
E;eeeef!
Autumn, a prayer I chant at sunset!
E;eeeef!
Autumn, a new art, a color of sunrise!

Hills of autumn
D# D# fe
My autumn bells, an autumn
D# d# d # d# fee
An autumn sunrise, an autumn!
D# d# d# d# d# d#, edd
An autumn pumpkin an autumn!
D# d# d# d# d# d#, edd

Round and round and round,
My hills,
An autumn,
My sunrise prayers,
A sunrise, an autumn
An autumn
Hills of autumn

Grace, an ode to autumn hills!

E;eeeeef!
Prayers, an ode to an autumn temple!
E: eeeeeef!
Autumn, A flower I bestow every!
E;eeeeef!

Square and square and square
My hills,
An autumn,
Hills of autumn…

Autumn, my autumn prayers an autumn!

Autumn, my autumn flowers
Flowers, an autumn!

Hills of autumn!
D# D# fe
Round and round
My meadows, an autumn!
D#d#d# fe
A Square and square
An art, my cottage!
D# d# d# fe
angle and angle and angle
A grace, my hills!

Hills of autumn
D#d#; fe
A praise of autumn
D#d#d# fe
An ode to an autumn !
D# d# d# fe

Hills of Autumn
A praise of Autumn
An ode to
An autumn!

DURGA MADIRAJU...

MBA, MS Information Systems, MA Economics
PhD Business Administration (Thesis)
Advanced Diploma in German
Certified in Executive and High Performance Leadership - Cornell University
Certified in Executive Business and Data Analytics - MIT
Certified Scrum Master (CSM)
Certified Six Sigma Green Belt, Growth,
Lean Certified
Quality by Design Certified
Presidential Voluntary Service Award (2014-2016)

Member Voluntary Committees: AT&T

- WOA (Women of Atlanta) – Mentoring Committee 2009-2017
- APCA Judge (Asian Pacific Islanders for Professional and Community Advancement)
- Oxygen Mentor 2012-2017
- PAC (Political Action Committee) Ambassador 2013-2017
- OASIS Member 2012-2017
- Member of Technology Inventions and Process Improvements (AT&T) 2009-2017

Certificates and Awards at AT&T

- IT Wall of Stars 2011
- IT professional Growth Award 2010
- Technology Development Award 2012
- Six Sigma Green Belt Growth Award 2009

Marquis Awards

Marquis Who's Who World 2021
Marquis Who's Who's America 2018-19
Marquis Who's Who Lifetime Achievement Award 2021
Marquis Who's Who Humanitarian Award 2021
Marquis Who's Who Top Engineer Award 2020

Marquis Who's Who Industry Leader Award 2021
Power Of Women of Excellence Award 2018-2019

Publications:

- Article publication: Agile, A Quality Metric Tool – Scrum Alliance
- Poetry – Jane Summers Poetry Classics
- Seasonal Woods, Jane Summers – Vol 1
- Summer Woods, Jane Summers – Vol 2
- Autumn Woods, Jane Summers – Vol 3
- Winter Woods, Jane Summers – Vol 4
- A View To A Door Vol 1

Printed in the United States
by Baker & Taylor Publisher Services